Ministry of Education
Information Services
13th Floor, Mowat Block, Queen's Park
Toronto M7A 1L2

An Overview of Canadian Education

Fourth Edition

---

by Margaret Gayfer

Canadian Education Association/
Association canadienne d'éducation
Suite 8-200, 252 Bloor Street West, Toronto, Ontario
M5S 1V5

1991

© Canadian Education Association/
Association canadienne d'éducation
First edition 1974
Second edition 1978; reprinted 1979
Third edition 1984
Fourth edition 1991

ISBN: 0-920315-50-X

Printed in Canada

Cover by MonaChrome Design

Publié en français sous le titre :
Un aperçu de l'éducation au Canada

CONTENTS

Chapter 1 - Some Basic Facts and Figures   1

    General Structure and Diversity   2
    The Federal Government   3

Chapter 2 -Provincial/Territorial Structure   5

    Departments of Education   6
    Financing   7
    Separate Schools   8
    Supervision   9
    School Year   9
    School Attendance   10
    Textbooks   10
    Curriculum   12
    Diplomas and Examinations   13
    Language in Education   15
    Multiculturalism   17

Teacher Qualifications and Training	19
Women in Education	20
Teacher Negotiations	21
The School Board	22
Public Participation	23

Chapter 3 - The Schools 25

Elementary Schools	26
Secondary Schools	27
Private Schools	28
Special Education	29
Education of Native People	30
Post-secondary Education	32
Post-secondary Financing	33
Universities	34
Community Colleges	36
Trade and Vocational Training	38
Continuing Education	40

Appendix 43

Departments of Education	43
Some Federal Departments	44
Some Federal Agencies	46
National Education Organizations	48
Further Reading	57

Quick Facts about Education in Canada

Figures from *1990-91 Advance Statistics of Education*, and from *Minority and Second Language Education, Elementary and Secondary Levels 1988-89*, Statistics Canada

Enrolment

Pre-elementary (kindergarten and nursery)	477,500
Elementary and secondary students	4,649,100
Community college students	324,420
University students	532,100
Total number of students	5,983,120

Number of Teachers

Elementary and secondary teachers	286,375
Community college teachers	25,890
University teachers	37,680
Total number of teachers	349,945

Number of Schools

Elementary and secondary schools	15,507
Community colleges and technical schools	201
Universities	69
Total	15,777

Finance-Cost of Education

Elementary-secondary	$29,300,626,000
Community college	$3,817,162,000
University	$9,714,242,000
Vocational Training	$3,648,810,000
Total expenditure	$46,480,840,000
Percentage of Gross Domestic Product spent on education in 1989-90	6.8%

Minority Language Education - Publicly Supported Schools

Number of French language minority schools	532
Minority French language enrolment*	154, 284
Number of English language minority schools	177
Minority English language enrolment	106, 271

Population (1986 census)

English as mother tongue	15.7 million
62.1%	
French as mother tongue	6. 4 million
25.1%	
Other languages as mother tongue	3. 2 million
12.8%	
Total population	25.3 million
Number of provinces	10
Number of territories	2
Total number of departments/ ministries of education	12

* Includes enrolment in all minority French language schools and in minority French language programs in other publicly supported schools.

Chapter 1

SOME BASIC FACTS AND FIGURES

SOME SIX million students were enrolled full-time in Canada's $46.5 billion educational enterprise during 1990-91. The number includes 5, 126, 600 (kindergarten to grade 12) students in elementary and secondary schools, 324, 400 in community colleges, and 532, 100 in universities.[1] The addition of those studying part-time (nearly 500,000 at the post-secondary level) and of the over 3.2 million in various types of adult education programs brings the total number of Canadians taking part in education to 9.3 million of the country's 26.4 million population. Canada spends a higher proportion of its Gross Domestic Product on public education than do Japan, U.S. or the U.K.

This learning force is served by a system of 15,507 elementary and secondary schools, 69 universities and 201 community colleges and technical institutes across Canada's ten provinces and two northern territories. There are close to 350,000 full-time teachers: 286,400 in the elementary and secondary school system, 37,700 in universities, and 25,900 in community colleges. Over the 1976-86 decade, the median number of years of formal schooling of the adult population rose from 11.3 to 12.2. By 1988, the proportion of adults with post-secondary credentials stood at 24.6%, up from 21.0% in 1984.[2]

---

1. Statistics Canada, *Advance Statistics of Education 1990-91* (Ottawa: Supply and Services Canada, 1990).

2. Statistics Canada, *Education in Canada. A Statistical Review for 1988-89* (Ottawa: Supply and Services Canada, 1990).

Canada's land mass of 9.970 million square kilometres makes it the second largest country in the world, second to the Soviet Union, and covering an area almost as large as Europe. Over 30% of the population lives in the metropolitan areas of the three largest cities: Toronto (3.4 million), Montreal (2.9 million), and Vancouver 1.4 million). The capital city, Ottawa, is in the province of Ontario. English and French are the official languages. English is the mother tongue of 62.1% of the population, and French of 25.1%. Nine out of ten francophones live in Quebec, where they make up 82.8% of the population. Of the 12.8% whose mother tongue is other than French or English, 2.1 million speak a language of European origin, 634,000 of Asian or Middle Eastern origin.[3]

General Structure and Diversity

The *Constitution Act* of 1867, which established a federal union of provinces, placed education "exclusively" under the control of each provincial legislature. This authority is confirmed in the *Constitution Act* of 1982. These exclusive powers are subject to certain reservations respecting the rights and privileges of denominational and minority schools in existence when each province was admitted to the Canadian confederation. Thus, the *Act* ratified the systems that already existed in Ontario, Quebec, New Brunswick and Nova Scotia. The six provinces that were admitted later (including Newfoundland and Labrador in 1949) were able to establish their own education systems.

Although the Yukon and the Northwest Territories are under the jurisdiction of the federal government, they have increasing autonomy and legislative council powers roughly similar to those of provincial legislatures. Each is administered by a Commissioner appointed by the government and an elected council. Both control education through their own legislation and departments of education, and act as independent entities when dealing with the rest of Canada on education matters. In the Northwest Territories, 59% (30,530) of the population are of aboriginal origin; in the Yukon, 21% (4,900) have aboriginal origins.

In consequence, Canada has ten provincial education systems, plus those of the Yukon and the Northwest Territories, and no federal government office of education. In each province and

---

3. Statistics Canada, *Canada Year Book 1990: A Review of Economic, Social and Political Developments in Canada* (Ottawa: Supply and Services, 1989).

territory, a department (or ministry) of education implements government policy and legislation. *School Acts* or *Education Acts* create local units of administration, called school boards or districts, charged with the responsibility for operating the school system. The boards are under the control of members of the general public who, in most cases, are elected by public ballot and are thus known as "trustees" of the public.

Although the education systems in the provinces are similar in many respects, the differences reflect the circumstances of regions separated by great distances and of the diversity of the country's historical and cultural heritage. The European conquest and settlement of Canada created a linguistic and cultural diversity that has been predominantly Anglo-Saxon, French and Celtic.

The Federal Government

Although education is primarily a provincial responsibility, the federal government has assumed direct control over the education of persons beyond the bounds of provincial jurisdiction: native people, armed forces personnel and their families, and the inmates of federal penal institutions. The Department of Indian and Northern Affairs maintains schools on reserves for Indian and Inuit children or funds their attendance at provincial public schools. The Department of National Defence maintains schools for children of the armed forces stationed in Canada and overseas, and operates three degree-granting colleges that educate and train officer cadets and officers. For prison inmates, Correctional Services of Canada provides academic education from primary through post-secondary, vocational education in trades and professions at secondary and post-secondary levels, and special programs for the illiterate and under-educated.

The growth of education, both in size and importance, made it almost inevitable that the federal government would play some role in its development and financing. Many national policies have a direct impact on the education system, such as immigration, official languages programs, multiculturalism, and manpower training needs. Many departments have functions that include education and training, but they tend to be financial, such as the sponsorship by Employment and Immigration Canada of co-operative training-employment programs.

In some respects, the Department of the Secretary of State is Canada's unofficial office of education because of its role in the development, implementation and review of all federal policies and programs relating to education. For example, it administers the Canada Student Loans Program, the federal-provincial fiscal arrangements for post-secondary education, and the grants for minority language and second official language instruction at the elementary, secondary and post-secondary levels. Within its jurisdiction is the Department of Multiculturalism and Citizenship, whose programs include funds for citizenship and language instruction for immigrants, the promotion of human rights, support for voluntary organizations, and cost-sharing agreements with provinces and territories on their new initiatives in adult literacy.

Chapter 2

PROVINCIAL/TERRITORIAL STRUCTURE

THE PROVINCES and the two territories have a parliamentary system of government with a legislature in which the majority party forms a cabinet or executive council of elected members. The government has the legal, administrative and financial responsibility for public education from elementary school through post-secondary. Each province has a department of education headed by a minister who is an elected member of the cabinet or, in the case of the Yukon and Northwest Territories, a councillor. (Some provinces also have a minister responsible for post-secondary education.) The minister is directly responsible for the management and operation of the education system through the department (or ministry) of education. The policies and powers of the government are embodied in a *School* or *Education Act* and *University and College Acts*. Other duties and obligations are in Regulations made by the minister, which deal with the implementation of principles.

Generally, a department of education undertakes the following functions: supervision of elementary and secondary schools; provision of curriculum and school organization guidelines; approval of new courses and textbooks; financing; teacher certification; regulations for trustees and education officials of school boards, principals and teachers; research; and support services such as libraries, health and transportation.

The power of provinces and territories over education includes the power to delegate certain duties and responsibilities for the operation of the school system to sub-organizations of local units of administration, generally called school boards, which function as corporations and operate under the province's legislation. Provincial authorities determine the number and type of school boards, their boundaries, and the number of trustees elected by the public at large. Most legislation contains both compulsory and permissive directives for the operation of the school system. The duties delegated to trustees are mainly in the area of business management: school building and maintenance; the raising of money by local property assessment and distribution of grant money from the government; approval of the hiring, promotion and dismissal of teachers; and the provision of instruction and curriculum design. The boards assign certain duties to professional educators (directors or superintendents of education) who are responsible for the delegation of duties to teachers and principals.

The direct supervisory and inspection role of the departments of education has been greatly diminished by the increased autonomy in curriculum and supervision given to school boards. Although departments have an evaluation and research function, in most cases the focus is more on policy formulation and on a consultative and leadership role. Several provinces have ongoing advisory bodies to help the minister and the department by developing strategies for reform and by relaying public opinion.

Departments of Education

The minister of education has the overall authority, but the day-to-day operation of the department of education is delegated to a deputy minister, a civil servant who is usually a professional educator. He or she has the duties of advising the minister, supervising the workings of the department, enforcing regulations and providing continuity in educational policy.

The typical department is difficult to describe, but generally it is organized on the basis of two functions: administration and finance; and curriculum, evaluation and support services. The development of educational technology and of office data technology has been a common focus. Five provinces have separate ministries or departments for post-secondary education and training: Ontario (Ministry of Colleges and Universities); Quebec (Ministry of Higher Education and Science); British Columbia (Ministry of Advanced Education, Training and Technology); Alberta (Department of Advanced Education); and New Brunswick (Department of Advanced Education and Training). Other provinces have created divisions within departments of education to look after the post-secondary aspects: Saskatchewan (Post-secondary and Adult Education); Manitoba (Post-secondary, Adult and Continuing Education); Newfoundland (Post-secondary Education and of Industrial Training); the Yukon and Northwest Territories (Advanced Education).

Financing

The revenues of school boards come from two main sources: grants from provincial or territorial governments and local taxation, generally a real property tax. Government has become the unit that finances the basic education program, which includes instructional and maintenance expenditures, cost of student transportation, and the financing of school sites and buildings. Instructional costs, both salary and non-salary, make up about 60% of public school spending. A high degree of educational and fiscal equity among boards has been achieved by grant formulas of various types. This equity factor has been aided by the drastic reduction in the number of school jurisdictions over the years, and by the assessment of real property on a uniform basis throughout each province. Inequalities continue to exist in the ability of boards to finance expenditures above those of the basic programs recognized by the province, but the trend has been to restrict such expenditures to a small percentage of the total.

The proportion of school board revenues from provincial and territorial grants varies across Canada, as shown in the 1988-89 figures from Statistics Canada[1]: Newfoundland 92%; Prince Edward Island and New Brunswick 100%; Nova Scotia just over 80%; Quebec 92%; Ontario just over 40%; Manitoba 53%; Saskatchewan 51%; Alberta 56%; British Columbia 60%; Yukon 94%; and the Northwest Territories 95%.

The total expenditure on education from elementary through post-secondary for 1990-91 was estimated at $46.5 billion. According to Statistics Canada[2], government (federal, provincial and local)

---

1. Canadian Education Statistics Council, *A Statistical Portrait of Elementary and Secondary Education in Canada* (Ottawa: Statistics Canada and Toronto: Council of Ministers of Education, Canada, 1990), p. 55 and pp. 59-70.
2. Statistics Canada, *Advance Statistics of Education 1990-91* (Ottawa: Supply and Services Canada, 1990), p. 12 and tables 11 and 13.

continued to fund more than 90% of the total cost. The share of total funding directly from provincial governments remained relatively stable at between 63% and 64%. Direct financing from federal sources accounted for 9.8%, compared with 10.3% in 1987-88. (This excludes indirect contributions for post-secondary education and official languages in education programs.) The share from local government sources decreased from 18.0% in 1987-88 to 17.2% in 1990-91. The breakdown of total spending by level was: elementary-secondary 63%; post-secondary 29%; and vocational training 8.0%.

Separate Schools

Several provinces provide tax support to school boards on a denominational basis. *School Acts* in Quebec, Ontario, Saskatchewan, Alberta and the Northwest Territories give such support for elementary and secondary education in both public and separate (or, in Quebec, for dissentient) school boards. (The first tax-supported school established in an area is referred to as a public school. Separate schools are generally referred to as being Roman Catholic, although in a few cases they are Protestant.) In September 1985, Ontario extended its funding for Roman Catholic school boards from grade 10 to all secondary school grades. In Quebec, elementary and secondary public education operates a dual denominational system of Roman Catholic and Protestant school boards. Technically, this applies only to boards on the Island of Montreal and in Quebec City. Traditionally, Protestant school boards have been associated with the anglophone minority and Roman Catholic boards with the francophone majority.

In the Yukon, both public and Roman Catholic schools receive tax support. Newfoundland's legislation provides for a tax-supported system of educational districts established for a religious denomination or groups of denominations. A non-sectarian public education system operates in Manitoba, British Columbia, New Brunswick, Nova Scotia and Prince Edward Island.

New Brunswick has French and English school boards and schools throughout the province. Ontario has created two French-language boards and is developing criteria for setting up others. This is to implement the guarantee in the *Charter of Rights and Freedoms* (*Constitution Act* 1982) that children of English- and

French-speaking minorities can elect to be educated in their own language. Other provinces are also considering similar action.

Supervision

School boards usually select their own chief supervisory officer and pay him or her for the performance of duties set out in the appropriate *Act*. In some provinces the minister of education normally approves the person's professional qualifications and confirms the appointment; in others, the minister does not. The title for the position of chief executive officer varies, but the most common are superintendent of schools, superintendent, or director of education. In some provinces, such as British Columbia and Saskatchewan, the department of education may directly appoint the superintendent because of the small size or limited capacity of the board. In the Northwest Territories, the two Yellowknife boards appoint their superintendent, but directors of divisional boards are appointed directly by the department. Some provinces and territories appoint field officers or superintendents to evaluate schools, programs and teacher performance. However, this direct supervisory function of departments of education has lessened considerably, and such officials are often designated as consultants.

School Year

The school year for elementary and secondary schools is ten months, from late August or early September until the end of June. It consists of 180 to 200 teaching days from Monday to Friday. Some provinces allow school boards freedom to set opening and closing dates. All schools observe national and provincial statutory holidays. There are two longer holiday periods during the year: seven to ten days at Christmas and five days in the spring. The spring break is handled differently among the provinces. Some hold it whenever Easter falls; others have established a regular week in March. The academic year of universities usually starts after mid-September and continues until late April or early May; there are holiday periods at Christmas and in February or March.

The length of the school day can vary among provinces because legislation may give school boards flexibility in setting the hours of their school day. Variations are based on grade levels.

Kindergarten is usually a half day; sometimes the day is shorter in the early grades (1-3) than the higher grades. The school day usually begins at 9:00 a.m. and ends between 3:00 and 4:00 p.m., providing approximately five-and-a-half hours of instruction time.

School Attendance

Children are obliged by law to attend school from age 6 or 7 until age 15 or 16, which is normally grades 1 to 10. Education in the public co-educational system is free for Canadian citizens and permanent residents. The upper limit for free attendance varies between age 19 and 21. Quebec extends its free education to its community college system for students in full-time programs of at least four courses per semester. The age of compulsory attendance varies. The starting age of 6 applies in Newfoundland, Nova Scotia, Quebec, Ontario, Alberta, British Columbia and the Northwest Territories. Seven is the compulsory starting age in Prince Edward Island, New Brunswick, Manitoba, Saskatchewan and the Yukon. The minimum leaving age of 16 applies across the country, except in the Northwest Territories where the minimum leaving age is 15.

Textbooks

Each department of education publishes a list of textbooks approved for use in its schools under the authority of the minister of education. Preference is given to materials written by Canadians and manufactured in Canada. In Ontario, 95% of the texts on its Circular 14 list are Canadian. The school principal, with teachers, is responsible for selecting materials from the list. Permission from the minister to use unlisted texts and supplementary instructional materials is usually directed through the school board's chief educational officer. Most provinces have a free textbook program for all students from grade 1 to 12, subsidized by specific money included in the provincial grant scheme. Some provinces may charge secondary school students for special texts, at a 50% discount.

The Northwest Territories and all provinces except Ontario and Quebec purchase textbooks through a central office called the school book bureau or curriculum resources division. The bureau operates as an adjunct to the department of education. It purchases bulk shipments of the authorized texts and distributes them to the schools.

The Structure of Education in Canada

Each province has its own system for education and the structure can vary considerably from province to province. This chart illustrates the similarities and differences.

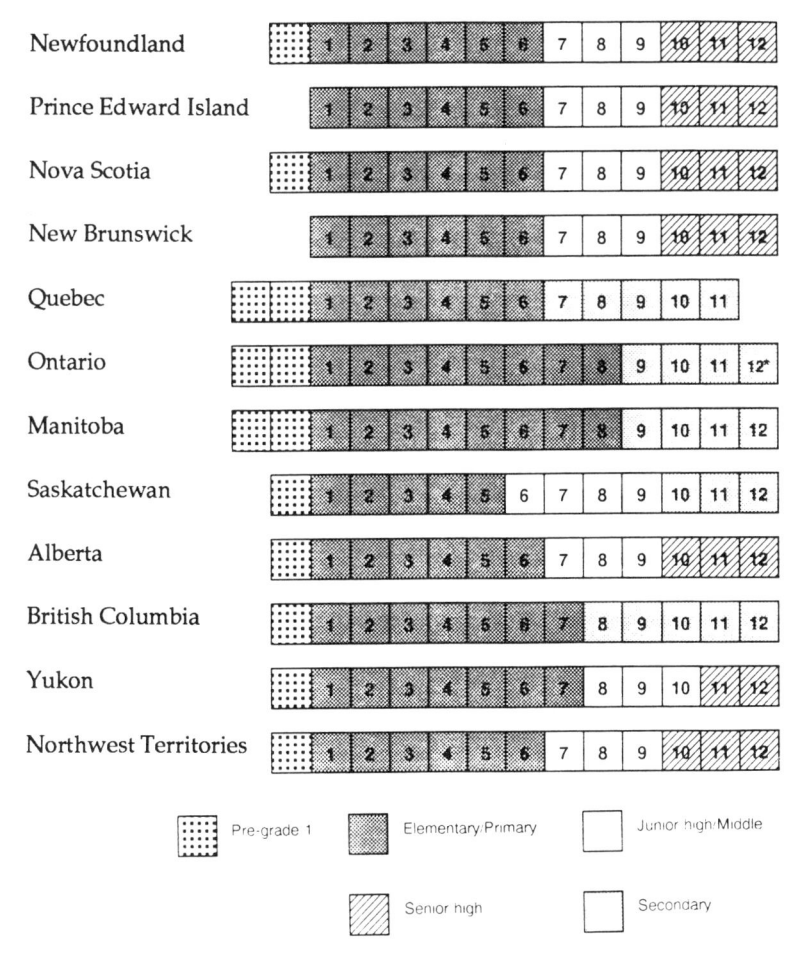

Newfoundland	Pre-grade 1 / 1–6 Elementary / 7–9 / 10–12 Senior high
Prince Edward Island	Pre-grade 1 / 1–6 Elementary / 7–9 / 10–12 Senior high
Nova Scotia	Pre-grade 1 / 1–6 Elementary / 7–9 / 10–12 Senior high
New Brunswick	1–6 Elementary / 7–9 / 10–12 Senior high
Quebec	Pre-grade 1 / 1–6 Elementary / 7–11
Ontario	Pre-grade 1 / 1–6 Elementary / 7–8 / 9–12*
Manitoba	Pre-grade 1 / 1–6 Elementary / 7–8 / 9–12
Saskatchewan	Pre-grade 1 / 1–5 Elementary / 6–8 / 9–12
Alberta	Pre-grade 1 / 1–6 Elementary / 7–9 / 10–12 Senior high
British Columbia	Pre-grade 1 / 1–7 Elementary / 8–12 Secondary
Yukon	Pre-grade 1 / 1–7 Elementary / 8–10 / 11–12 Senior high
Northwest Territories	Pre-grade 1 / 1–6 Elementary / 7–9 / 10–12 Senior high

Legend: Pre-grade 1 | Elementary/Primary | Junior high/Middle | Senior high | Secondary

*Includes Ontario Academic Credits (primarily for students completing university entrance courses)

Source: Canadian Education Statistics Council, *A Statistical Portrait of Elementary and Secondary Education, Canada* (Ottawa: Statistics Canada; Toronto: Council of Ministers of Education, Canada, 1990) C.S. 2-38/1990

Curriculum

The minister of education is responsible for prescribing courses of study which set out the content of the school program and the overall sequence in which it is taught. The minister authorizes which subjects are to be compulsory. Departments of education issue curriculum guidelines, which are general outlines of the course content. Supervisory officers of a school board are responsible for ensuring that particular courses of study are designed within the philosophy and approach of the guidelines; principals and sometimes teachers share in this duty.

The intent of current policy is that teachers, preferably as part of the school staff, take an active role in designing the courses they teach and in developing supplementary resource materials. Input from students, especially at senior levels, is also encouraged. School boards must seek ministerial approval for new courses, which are often developed locally. A new course is usually introduced and evaluated at more than one school before a decision is made to apply it province-wide.

Curriculum priorities include the following emphases: solid grounding in basic skills; core curricula; early childhood education and smaller class size for early grades; knowledge of science and technology; application of computers to curriculum and instruction; using techniques of distance education to improve the array of programs available to isolated and small schools; attention to AIDS in health education; and stricter regulations for the secondary school diploma by making more courses compulsory and specifying core subjects.

As the result of renewed interest in more systematic evaluation methods for the school system, in 1990, the Council of Ministers of Education, Canada, launched its national School Achievement Indicators Program to help provinces and territories to assess student achievement and identify priorities in education in a national context. One group of indicators describes involvement in the education system (rates of participation, retention and graduation). The second group gives information about the literacy and numeracy skills of students age 13 and 16, and the extent to which achievement increases between these ages. A sample of students across the country will be assessed using instruments in French and English.

Curriculum priorities have shown an increasing recognition of the role of education in preparing students for employment, and have resulted in a variety of school-to-work transition programs, co-operative work-study in partnership with business and industry, and emphasis on work experience and career preparation for students at risk. In early 1990, the federal Minister of Employment and Immigration announced a $296.4 million stay-in-school initiative to reduce the 30% dropout rate in Canadian high schools which results in some 100,000 young people a year entering the labour market without sufficient skills. The program has three major components: expansion of federal labour-market programs and services; mobilizing business, labour, educators and parents; and a national information program to raise public awareness of the dropout problem and to encourage young people to stay in school.

Diplomas and Examinations

During the past few years a number of provinces have been revising the core curriculum of secondary school programs and the number of credits and compulsory courses required for graduation. This has led to a new interest in compulsory provincial examinations for all or some courses for the school-leaving diploma. High school graduation is after 12 years of schooling in all provinces and territories except in Quebec where it is after 11 years.

British Columbia will have phased in its new framework for secondary schools by 1993-94. Graduation requires a total of 13 courses in grades 11 and 12, five of which are core courses and four authorized by the province. The province-wide exams required in grade 12 academic subjects form 40% of the final mark. The *Yukon* follows British Columbia's basic program as well as its graduation and examination system. In September 1988 *Alberta* introduced changes in requirements for the grade 12 diploma and changes are continuing until the senior high school programs have been completed. A minimum number of credits have been set for grades 10 to 12. Provincial exams are mandatory for the grade 12 diploma in certain core courses. The final mark is determined by averaging the mark given by the school with the exam mark. The *Northwest Territories* uses selected curricula from Alberta and follows Alberta's graduation diploma requirements.

Since September 1988 *Saskatchewan* has been implementing a new core curriculum for the entire school system. Students entering high school at grade 10 must acquire 24 credits (formerly 21) of which five must be at the grade 12 level. English is compulsory for grades 11 and 12 as are credits in social studies, science, social science and math. A minimum of two credits is required in arts education, practical and applied art, and health and physical education. Department of Education exams are required for grade 12 academic subjects if the teacher is not accredited in that subject. In 1990 *Manitoba* began a major reorganization of secondary school education which will be phased in over a period of four years. Key elements are province-wide standards and exams, a revised curricula, and more core subjects as compulsory credits. Students in the last two years are to write summative exams in all subjects. The introduction of province-wide exams in one major subject in the final year began with math in the 1990-91 school year.

By September 1991 all school boards in *New Brunswick* had started to implement the new credit system in senior high school programs, which will be completed by 1993-94. School boards have a choice of two programs. They may offer a 21-credit program with a minimum of 18 credits for graduation, of which 13 are compulsory, or a 24-credit program with a minimum of 20 credits, of which 14 are compulsory. Provincial exams for the grade 12 diploma are set only in the francophone school sector in order to verify student achievement in compulsory subjects. Since 1990 *Nova Scotia* has been redefining its high school credit system and the number of credits (up from 16 to 18) required for graduation. Required are three English credits (or three French credits for French-speaking students), two social studies, one each in French, math and science, one in fine arts and the equivalent of one credit in independent living and physically active life styles. In *Newfoundland*, graduation requires 21 credits in core subjects in four categories. All courses require a public exam and the final mark is determined through an evaluation shared by the school and the department of education. Graduation in *Prince Edward Island* requires 18 credits that include language arts, math, social studies and science. Five must be at the grade 12 level.

Students in *Quebec* enter the five-year secondary school program after six years of elementary school, usually at age 12. All courses passed since the beginning of secondary school count toward graduation. At least 130 units must be accumulated and 20 of these must be in Secondary V courses. By June 1995, graduation will require 30 Secondary V units instead of the present 20. The Quebec Ministry of Education sets certain exams in the last two years, some of which are compulsory for graduation. *Ontario* has replaced its two graduation diplomas for grades 12 and 13 by a single diploma awarded at the end of grade 12 for 30 credits including 16 compulsory ones. Grade 13 is replaced by the Ontario

Academic Course (OAC), which offers the six credits (which may be part of the necessary 30) required for university entrance.

Language in Education

The recognition in 1969 of French and English as Canada's official languages was followed by the federal government's Official Languages in Education Program. The objectives are to encourage and assist the provision of educational services in the minority official language in each province and territory and to provide opportunities for Canadians to learn their other official language. Later, under the *Constitution Act* of 1982, the *Charter of Rights and Freedoms* set out significant guarantees of minority language rights for elementary and secondary education according to three criteria: 1) mother tongue, 2) language in which parents were educated in Canada, and 3) language in which other children in the family are being or have been educated.[3] These criteria depend on there being enough eligible children in an area to warrant setting up school facilities out of public funds. The criteria apply everywhere except in Quebec where the first criterion of access by virtue of mother tongue does not apply. Under bilateral agreements, the federal government gives financial assistance to the provinces and territories for the additional costs they incur in developing and maintaining language services. In 1989-90, the contributions totalled $225.7 million. The allocation to minority language education was 63.8% (35.8% outside Quebec and 28.0% in Quebec; second language instruction received 36.2% (29.6% outside Quebec and 6.6% in Quebec)[4]

Based on definitions applied at the provincial level, the official minority language is English in Quebec and French elsewhere. However, New Brunswick is an officially bilingual province, where francophones are a third of the population. According to the 1986 census, nine out of ten Canadians with French as their only mother tongue lived in Quebec, where 82.2% reported French as their only mother tongue. The proportion of Quebec residents who spoke English at home was 12.2%. Some 945,860 persons

---

3. Government of Canada, *The Charter of Rights and Freedoms: A Guide for Canadians* (Ottawa: Supply and Services Canada, 1982), pp. 22 and 24.

4. Department of the Secretary of State of Canada, *Annual Report 1989-90 Official Languages* (Ottawa: Supply and Services Canada, 1991), p. 45.

whose mother tongue was French lived outside Quebec.[5]

Minority language programs offer instruction in the mother tongue for most of the school day. In schools outside Quebec students in pre-elementary to grade 8 generally spend 85% to 100% of the week on French. Those in grade 9 and up have French instruction for 65% to 75% of the week. *French immersion,* an option that flourishes particularly in larger urban areas, covers all grades and ranges from 100% immersion in early grades to 50% and 25% later on. In the *regular program,* students take the second language as a regular (core) subject. In several provinces, French is compulsory after grade 4 or 5. In Quebec, English is a compulsory subject in the French system from grade 4 through graduation.[6]

All provinces and territories are represented in the 76% of public schools outside Quebec with minority and second language programs. Over 1.9 million students in English schools were enrolled in French second language (regular and immersion) programs in 1988-89. Of these, close to 90% were in the regular program. Some 12% of all second language students were enrolled in French immersion programs. In 1988-89, some 154,284 students were in French minority programs in 532 schools. That year Quebec had 177 schools with minority English programs. Enrolment has declined steadily in these programs to 106,271 because of Quebec's declining birthrate and legislation that requires children whose mother tongue was neither French nor English to attend French schools.[7]

At elementary school, participation rates in second language education ranged, in 1988-89, from 97% in New Brunswick, 70% in Ontario, 61% in Saskatchewan and Manitoba, to 28% in the Northwest Territories. Participation in secondary school second language programs was highest in Quebec (100%), followed by over 50% in Manitoba, Saskatchewan and the Yukon, and 40% in Ontario.[8]

New Brunswick guarantees French- and English-speaking

---

5. Statistics Canada, *Canada Year Book 1990. A Review of Economic, Social and Political Developments in Canada* (Ottawa: Supply and Services, 1989), pp. 2-5 to 2-7.

6. Statistics Canada, *Minority and Second Language Education, Elementary and Secondary Levels 1988-89* (Ottawa: Supply and Services Canada, 1990); and Canadian Education Statistics Council, *A Statistical Portrait of Elementary and Secondary Education, Canada, op. cit.,* pp. 26-28.

7. Statistics Canada, *Minority and Second Language Education, op. cit.*

8. Statistics Canada, *Education in Canada: A Statistical Review for 1988-89* (Ottawa: Supply and Services Canada, 1990), p. 40.

pupils instruction in their own language. Its legislation provides for minority-language school boards in school districts that had been established originally on the basis of the language of the majority. In British Columbia, Saskatchewan, Manitoba, Ontario, Nova Scotia and Prince Edward Island, legislation guarantees the right to French-language schooling where numbers are sufficient. In 1984, Ontario revised its legislation so that school boards are required to extend French-language education to francophone students regardless of numbers. In Quebec, the right to English-language education is guaranteed according to specific criteria for those who qualify. Newfoundland's policy statement recognizes the linguistic right of francophone students where numbers warrant. In Alberta, permissive legislation allows school boards to use French as a language of instruction.

Increased attention has been given to the right of francophones to manage and control French-language schools and school boards. In 1986, Ontario provided minority language groups with the right to govern their own schools or instructional units within existing school boards, and has developed criteria for the governance of additional French-language boards. Saskatchewan is implementing a management system for French schools through school councils of parents, and Manitoba has set up a task force on the governance issue.

Multiculturalism

Canada's multiculturalism policy, introduced in 1971, is an integrationist strategy. It is based on the belief that people's confidence in their own identity and place in the Canadian mosaic makes it easier for them to accept the rights of members of other groups in the society. The policy does not aim to maintain different cultural systems but to preserve as much of ethnic cultures as is compatible with Canadian customs.[9] The Canadian *Multiculturalism Act* [10] of 1988 recognizes the racial and cultural diversity of Canadians. It states that every Canadian has the freedom to enjoy, enhance and share her or his heritage, and that all Canadians must have equal opportunities and must be treated with the same respect.

---

9   Economic Council of Canada, *New Faces in the Crowd. Economic and Social Impacts of Immigration* (Ottawa: Supply and Services Canada, 1991), p. 32.

10.   Multiculturalism and Citizenship Canada, *Operation of the Canadian Multiculturalism Act: Annual Report 1989-90* (Ottawa: Supply and Services Canada, 1991).

Most departments of education across the country have guidelines or policies for school boards to develop policies and curricula for promoting multiculturalism, human rights, citizenship and cross-cultural understanding and, in five provinces, for offering instruction in heritage languages.

The multiculturalism policy is a response to successive changes in immigration legislation since the 1960s. During the 1980s, 1.25 million people immigrated to Canada. About one-third were of European origin; the remainder came from Asia, Africa, Latin America and the Caribbean. By 1986, approximately 16% of the population had come as immigrants, and more than one-third did not speak either English or French.[11] Even though the number of immigrants has increased sharply, by 1988 the immigrant population under age 18 represented less than 1% of the total population for that age group. However, immigration has an impact on certain school districts because of its concentration in a few provinces and, within them, in the major urban areas. An influx of students from different cultural backgrounds means that many school boards have had to start new or expand programs in English or French as a second language and for orientation and counselling.

In 1988, Ontario received 55% of all immigrant children, Quebec 17%, British Columbia 13%, Alberta 8.5%, and Manitoba 3%. The other provinces and territories accounted for just under 3% in total. Some 70% of all immigrant children went to six cities: Toronto, Montreal, Vancouver, Edmonton, Calgary and Winnipeg. About 60% went to the first three cities; 35% to Toronto alone. Patterns of residence show that cities in western Canada received a higher proportion of immigrants unable to speak English or French (71%) than did Toronto (62%) and Montreal (64%).[12]

The response of the school system to the philosophy of multiculturalism and the cultural and linguistic diversity of much of Canadian society has been the development, not without controversy, of heritage language programs. The term usually refers to all modern languages other than aboriginal ones and English or French, although some jurisdictions may include aboriginal languages in their definition.

A survey of school boards by the Canadian Education Association,[13] found that heritage language programs exist in many

---

11. Economic Council of Canada, *New Faces in the Crowd*, op. cit.
12. Canadian Education Statistics Council, *A Statistical Portrait of Elementary and Secondary Education, Canada*, op. cit., p. 16.
13. Canadian Education Association, *Heritage Language Programs in Canadian School Boards* (Toronto: CEA, 1991).

school boards in Quebec, Ontario, Manitoba, Saskatchewan and Alberta, and are being planned by British Columbia. Legislation is permissive, leaving the decision to institute such courses to the school boards, except in Ontario. Its 1989 legislation there made such programs mandatory in elementary schools where the request for a language is made by parents of 25 or more of the students under the board's jurisdiction. These classes in Ontario are held during out-of-school hours.

The extent of the involvement of school boards in the five provinces depends upon the underlying legislation, ethnic groups, and policies and funding from the department of education. Programs range from the smallest (one class) to classes in 72 Quebec schools in a variety of languages and to Ontario's 96,000 students in 4500 classes in 68 school boards in 62 different languages. Almost every language in the world, from Arabic through to Vietnamese, is taught somewhere in Canada. With a few exceptions, heritage language programs are offered only in the elementary grades. Scheduling varies: for some boards the program is a normal part of the school day; others use a bilingual format, and still others place it after school, in the evenings, at weekends or as an extension of the school day. The total weekly time allotted to the programs also varies, but the range is generally from 100 to 150 minutes per week.

Teacher Qualifications and Training

An estimated 1% increase in the number of full-time elementary and secondary school teachers in 1990-91 brings their number to 286,400. In 1988-89 there were 27,200 part-time teachers, which is equivalent to 15,900 full-time teachers.[14] The department (or ministry) of education grants certificates only to those who comply with its regulations, which vary from province to province.[15] Only the minister of education can suspend or cancel a certificate. In all provinces, with one exception, training for both elementary and secondary teachers is conducted by faculties of education within universities. Nova Scotia Teachers' College has a degree program, in which the education degree is awarded jointly with a university.

14. Statistics Canada, *Advance Statistics of Education 1990-91, op. cit.*, p. 10; and Statistics Canada, *Education in Canada: A Statistical Review for 1988-89, op. cit.*, p. 194.
15. See *Requirements for Teaching Certificates in Canada*, (Toronto: Canadian Education Association, 1987).

In the last two decades nearly all those admitted into the teaching profession have held university degrees. In-service professional training and higher levels of certification beyond the basic certificate include updating and acquiring additional qualifications usually through courses offered by departments of education, school boards and faculties of education. Courses and workshops are also offered by teachers' associations and associations of education and administrative officials.

In 1991, Newfoundland, Nova Scotia, Prince Edward Island, New Brunswick and Manitoba agreed to implement the same policy on the portability of teachers' certificates. This agreement allows teachers trained in one of these five provinces to transfer and be eligible to teach in the other four provided the following requirements are met: 1) a valid teaching certificate issued by one of the five provincial departments of education; 2) a three- or four-year degree awarded by a university that is an ordinary member of the Association of Universities and Colleges of Canada (or any equivalent degree acceptable to the receiving province) and 3) one year (or equivalent) of teacher training completed in one of the named five provinces and recognized by that province's department of education.

In 1983, the Department of Education of the Northwest Territories began issuing its own certificates to teachers employed in its schools. In 1990, the Yukon's *Teaching Profession Act* formally established and recognized teaching as a profession, as does similar legislation throughout Canada. The two territories and several provinces have been putting an emphasis on different kinds of teacher education opportunities for native people (see the section in Chapter 3 on Education of Native People).

Women in Education

The situation of women and men in positions within educational systems across Canada reflects tradition, rather than employment equity, according to a survey of gender distribution in school systems, undertaken by the Canadian Education Association.[16] That survey showed that women do hold positions of responsibility within school boards, but that these are mainly staff

---

16. Ruth Rees, *Women and Men in Education. A National Survey of Gender Distribution in School Systems* (Toronto: Canadian Education Association, 1990).

positions in supportive and consultative roles. Not many women are in line/supervisory positions of authority within the system nor are they represented in positions of added responsibility in proportion to their gender representation within education as a whole.

The pattern in the schools is similar to that at the school boards: men dominate as managers and administrators, and women emerge and lead in staff positions, such as classroom teachers, curriculum resource teachers, special education teachers. Men are in the majority as principals, vice-principals and department heads at secondary schools, junior high and elementary schools. Men compose most of the teachers at the secondary school. Although women compose 60% to 80% of the teaching force in elementary schools across the provinces, they are still a minority in the management of these schools. Women account for 15% to 38% of principals, and fewer than 50% are vice-principals. Section or department heads are usually men.

Teacher Negotiations

Negotiations on all matters are conducted with the provincial government in New Brunswick, Prince Edward Island, and Newfoundland. In Quebec, teacher negotiations are for the most part conducted at the provincial level but arrangements at the local level are also made. In the Northwest Territories, teachers in the two Yellowknife school boards negotiate with the boards, but all other teachers negotiate with the government. Yukon teachers negotiate with the government. In British Columbia, negotiations are conducted both at the local and zonal level, but the government intends to introduce provincial bargaining soon (1992-93) for B.C. teachers. In Alberta they are held at the local and regional level. Manitoba and Ontario teachers negotiate at the school board level except for the six Metro Toronto school boards (East York, Etobicoke, North York, Scarborough, Toronto, York) and the Metropolitan Toronto School Board which negotiate jointly with branch affiliate representatives of teachers' federations from each school board. In Nova Scotia and Saskatchewan, negotiations occur both at the local and provincial levels.

The usual route to agreement is through negotiation, conciliation and arbitration. When conciliation fails, arbitration is compulsory and binding in Manitoba and available on request of either party in Prince Edward Island. Voluntary arbitration by agreement of both parties is available to teachers in Newfoundland, Nova Scotia, New Brunswick, Quebec (local level), Ontario, Saskatchewan, the Northwest Territories and Yukon. Teacher strikes are permitted in the Yukon, British Columbia, Alberta, Saskatchewan, Ontario, Quebec, New Brunswick, Nova Scotia (provincial level only), and Newfoundland.

British Columbia's *Teaching Profession Act* of 1987 was the first legislation of its kind in Canada to give teachers the right of self-regulation as a profession through the establishment of a College of Teachers. Teachers have full rights to collective bargaining and had the option to bargain as either a non-union teachers' federation or as a certified union with the right to strike.

The School Board

The issue of local control of education in the face of increasing centralized control by provincial governments goes back to pioneer days when communities built their own schools and hired their own teachers. From the 1960s on, small school boards have been consolidated into central, regional or county districts large enough to achieve a degree of equality in educational services for the elementary and secondary schools within their jurisdictions. The management of the school system is the legal responsibility of school boards, most of which are now composed entirely of publicly elected "lay" trustees or commissioners. However, boards are creatures of the provinces because they exist under legislation that determines and delegates their powers.

Generally, the school board handles the business aspects that keep the system functioning, including setting the annual budget, establishing policies to be implemented by professional educators, appointing teachers, capital building, and purchase of supplies and equipment. Most boards are authorized to levy taxes or to requisition taxes from municipal governments and to manage grants from the department of education.

The persistence of the issue of local control shows in the separation of municipal and educational governance in most parts of Canada, which comes from the desire to separate education from

---

17. Stephen B. Lawton, *The Price of Quality: The Public Finance of Elementary and Secondary Education in Canada* (Toronto: Canadian Education Association, 1987), p. 12.

all property-holders and tenants within the board's boundaries. The number of trustees per board is usually based on student enrolment. Some provinces hold trustee elections at the same time as municipal elections; some others hold them separately. In still other provinces, a certain number of trustees are elected annually on an "overlap" formula. The term of office is generally two or three years.

A trustee's job has traditionally been regarded as part-time, a community service with no salary or a small honorarium. Many trustees take seriously their role as a representative of the public, and encourage parent and community involvement in school affairs. Particularly in urban centres with large school populations, there is a growing trend in the thinking that the demands on a trustee's time require a commensurate salary. The yearly salary varies from $45,000 in Toronto, $18,000 in Vancouver, $15,000 in Edmonton, to $7,680 in Montreal, and $6,000 in Halifax. In some areas, members of the school board receive no honorarium or are paid according to the number of board meetings they attend.[18]

Exceptions to the general form of school board governance are the two-tier systems for Metropolitan Toronto and for the Island of Montreal, Canada's largest cities. Six school boards form the Metropolitan Toronto School Board which allocates finances for each board following a study of their budgets. The Montreal Island School Council operates in a similar two-tier way for its eight district boards.

Public Participation

School boards and individual schools continue to seek ways for parents to take part in their children's education and for the public to be involved in educational issues. Many schools have community-parent advisory bodies and many boards have consultative committees that include parents and other members of the community. It's only natural, however, that participation is most active around a particular issue that affects the students' school life, such as a change in the curriculum or a reorganized structure. Recent samplings of public opinion showed mixed reactions to parental and public involvement. The Canadian Education Asso-

---

18. "$45,000 for trustees a 'horrendous' salary ex-minister says," *The Toronto Star*, 06 November 1989, sec. A13.

ciation's 1990 poll suggested an overall satisfaction with Canadian schools. On the report card for the responsiveness of schools to parents' concerns schools received A or B marks from 58% of respondents. (Some 83% gave schools an A, B or C.) The findings also indicated that elementary schools are more responsive to parents than secondary schools.[19] In an Ontario survey, 60% said that the general public has too little say in how schools are run, and 52% found a class bias against students from working class families.[20]

No province has legislation that prohibits schools or school boards from setting up community councils or parent advisory committees. Permissive legislation in some provinces enables a school board to establish advisory committees of teachers, school trustees, parents and community agencies. In 1989, the new *School Act* in British Columbia included the establishment of parent advisory councils at the school level. Quebec is the only province that makes mandatory the setting up of school councils to which parents are elected. Delegates from each council form a parents' committee for the school board as a permanent liaison between the board and the school councils.

Most provincial departments of education are concerned with gathering public input and opinion. They seek public opinion through task forces, advisory or review committees, parliamentary commissions, discussing and reviewing papers and by commissioning surveys. In some provinces, formal consultative bodies to advise the minister have been set up.

---

19. Tom R. Williams and Holly Millinoff, *Canada's Schools: Report Card for the 1990s: A CEA Opinion Poll* (Toronto: Canadian Education Association, 1990), p.18.

20. D. Livingstone, D. Hart and L.E. Davie, *Public Attitudes Towards Education in Ontario - 1990: Eighth OISE Survey*, in *Orbit*, April 1991, p. 21 and 13.

Chapter 3

THE SCHOOLS

EARLY CHILDHOOD EDUCATION has been increasingly recognized as setting an important foundation for a child's further learning. There are two publicly supported and voluntary preschool systems that operate in most provinces and territories. One is usually called kindergarten, a pre-grade 1 program operated by school boards for children aged 5. The second system comprises licensed day care centres and nurseries which come under the jurisdiction of a provincial government department of social or community services, or of a special office.

All provinces and territories have kindergartens for five-year-olds, except Prince Edward Island, but it has an early childhood education component in its day care program. However, instead of the traditional kindergarten, Alberta has a unique, province-wide program called Early Childhood Services, which started in 1974. It mainly enrols children of four-and-a-half years of age (although children may be admitted a year earlier). About 95% of children aged four-and-a-half are now in centres run by school boards, private schools and operators of private ECS centres. The program seeks to integrate many aspects of child development by combining education, health, social and recreational services. The policy is to maintain continuity through to grade 6.

Some provinces have added a junior kindergarten year for children age four. Both senior and junior kindergarten may be a half or full day. In many provinces, this decision is made by the school board, in response to requests by parents. Although kindergarten is not compulsory, attendance has become the norm. For example, in Ontario, enrolment in junior kindergarten accounts for 40% of the overall growth in elementary and secondary enrolment since 1985. Pre-elementary enrolment has shown an upward trend since 1978-79. The growth is partly due to more children in preschool programs and to an increase in the age four and five population. Enrolment for pre-elementary classes in 1990-91 is estimated at 477, 490 (448, 140 in public schools, 19, 120 in private schools, and 10, 230 in federal schools).[1]

Day care programs are often located in an elementary school and provide services for pre-school children from 7:30 a.m. to 6:00 p.m. and for school-age children after school hours. Such programs are licensed under the appropriate provincial *Act*, are run as non-profit organizations, and are often initiated by parents. Quebec is the only province where legislation allows school boards to hold a day care permit and authorizes them to provide care for children in out-of-school hours.

Elementary Schools

Elementary usually refers to schools that offer kindergarten or grade 1 to grade 6 or 8 (children aged 5 or 6 to 11 or 13); secondary refers to schools with programs leading to and including the final year of graduation. The point of transition from elementary to secondary may vary from province to province (see chart on page 11). Some school boards break up the elementary-secondary continuum into schools that group certain grades: for example, kindergarten to grade 6 (elementary), grades 7-9 (junior high school), and grades 10-12 (senior high). Most schools are co-educational. The average enrolment in an elementary school is 250 pupils; only 17% of Canada's elementary schools have 400 or more students.

Elementary school curriculum concentrates on an interdisciplinary and broad orientation to basic learning in reading, writing and math, plus science, social studies, health education, music and art. Most provinces and territories have adopted some form of non-graded continuous progress by which students proceed to the next level of learning in a subject rather than, as in the past, repeat a full year in all subjects if their performance was not adequate in one or two subjects.

---

1. Statistics Canada, *Advance Statistics of Education 1990-91* (Ottawa: Supply and Services Canada, 1990), p. 21.

A significant development, particularly in the elementary school, is the rapid growth of the multi-grade classroom as an organizational unit in which two consecutive grades (rarely three) are combined under one teacher. The number of such classrooms, which are also called split or double classes, has increased dramatically across all types of school boards, especially those in urban areas because in recent years enrolments have fluctuated so much. A recent study by the Canadian Education Association[2] found that one out of seven classrooms in Canada is multi-grade, and that approximately one out of every five students is enrolled in such a classroom. The highest number of multi-grades occurs in elementary schools, specifically between grades 1 and 6. The study also found that children in multi-grade classes do just as well in cognitive and psycho-social development as their counterparts in single-grade classes.

Secondary Schools

To provide for different needs and abilities, the secondary (high school) level usually offers a choice of at least two programs: academic and vocational. In urban areas, some schools may specialize in vocational training (technical and commercial). However, most secondary schools are composite and offer both academic courses (generally, preparatory to university or community college) and vocational courses, which prepare students for an occupation or further training at a public trade or vocational school or at a community college. The system in Quebec is unique. The secondary school program (up to grade 11) is followed by an intermediate level of two or three years at a college of general and vocational education (*collège d'enseignement général et professionnel* or cégep). The two-year general program leads normally to university; students in the three-year option follow a career and vocational program leading to employment.

Secondary schools tend to be larger than elementary ones. Enrolment in just over half of Canada's 3,235 secondary schools is 400 students or more; the average size is 600 students. Schools are mainly organized around subject disciplines and students change

---

2. Joel Gajadharsingh, *The Multi-grade Classroom: Myth and Reality. A Canadian Study* (Toronto: Canadian Education Association, 1991).

classrooms to take courses from different teachers. Students must successfully complete a specified number of credits to receive a diploma. Departments of education establish the credit requirements, which include core and compulsory subjects. In recent years, a number of provinces have tightened their requirements (introducing more compulsory subjects) for a secondary school diploma; some have introduced various forms of compulsory province-wide examinations (see Diploma and Examinations, page 13). Students also select options or elective subjects for credit. The wide choice has produced a system of individualized timetabling and credit promotion by subject rather than by year-end grade. This flexibility means that many schools operate on a two-semester system, particularly at senior grade levels.

Graduation from a secondary school leads a student to employment, a trade school, community college or university.

Private Schools

Private schools, known as independent schools in most provinces outside of Quebec, serve to complement the public and separate school systems in every province. They are independent from the public system, but must provide programs of study that meet the provincial goals of basic education. In most cases, they follow the curriculum and diploma requirements of their province's department or ministry of education, although in some provinces they are free to offer alternatives that reflect the philosophy or pedagogy of the community they serve. In every province and territory independent schools may grant provincial diplomas provided they meet the provincial standards and regulations.

There are many types of independent schools and their objectives vary. Some serve specific religious communities, others provide programs based on specific pedagogies such as Montessori or Waldorf schools. There are schools that stress academic excellence or the development of talents in the performing arts. In the past, independent schools provided leadership in meeting the needs of exceptional students (gifted, physically or mentally handicapped, emotionally disturbed, etc.), and a significant number of schools continue to provide such services, often under contracts with public school authorities.

Independent schools usually charge fees because they do not have access to the same levels of funding as the public schools. A large proportion of the schools have bursary or tuition relief programs to subsidize the enrolment of children whose parents cannot afford the full costs. The schools' enrolment policies generally reflect those of special programs within the public and separate education systems in that they are designed to admit all students within the supporting faith or all students who are likely to benefit from the program.

Enrolment in the independent schools has always fluctuated between 2% and 6% of the total student population. In 1983-84, an estimated 4.7% of Canada's total elementary and secondary school enrolment was accounted for by 1,150 independent schools. In 1990-91, approximately 253,000 students, enrolled in 1,375 independent schools, make up 5.4% of the total student population. With 118,382 students in 280 independent schools, Quebec has the highest percentage of independent school enrolments (10%). This is followed by British Columbia and Manitoba, with 7.1% and 5% respectively. Neither British Columbia nor Manitoba have separate school systems and therefore the independent schools in those provinces include large numbers of Catholic schools.

Five provinces - British Columbia, Alberta, Saskatchewan, Manitoba and Quebec - provide some form of financial assistance to independent schools. Although the Maritime provinces have no provisions for funding independent schools, Prince Edward Island provides financial assistance for the purchase of authorized textbooks, and Nova Scotia gives independent schools access to authorized texts and learning materials through the Nova Scotia School Book Bureau. Newfoundland provides no funds for the operation of independent schools, but if the independent school is the only school in a community, it is required to operate as a public school and receives full public funding.

Special Education

All provinces and territories continue to give high priority to the provision of programs and services for students who are exceptional in their special learning requirements. This includes the physically handicapped, the learning disabled, the mildly handicapped, the emotionally disturbed and the educable or trainable mentally retarded. Gifted and talented children are also defined as exceptional. The philosophy of moving children out of special schools and integrating as many as possible into the public school system began with the common practice of starting special education classes within schools. The trend in recent years is to work closely with parents to integrate exceptional children into the classroom with children of their own age.

With the shift of responsibility for the education of exceptional children to departments of education, all provinces have taken steps, either in policy directives or in legislation, to ensure that special education is available to students who need it. Some provinces, such as Ontario, Newfoundland, Saskatchewan, Nova Scotia and Quebec, have legislation that requires school boards to provide such programs. In 1991, Alberta also developed plans for the co-ordination of services, funding and inter-agency co-operation.

A total of 21 schools either for the sight or hearing handicapped (blind or deaf) are directly administered by the provinces. Under the Atlantic Provinces Special Education Authority, Newfoundland, Nova Scotia, New Brunswick and Prince Edward Island jointly finance and operate two separate educational institutions in Nova Scotia for children with sight and hearing handicaps. Most provinces also operate schools or programs for the trainable retarded, for those in care, under treatment and in correctional facilities.

Education of Native People

According to the 1986 census, 711,725 persons (3% of the total population) had at least one parent of aboriginal origin. Of these, 40% gave a single North American Indian origin, 8.3% a single Métis origin (Indian and French), and 3.8% a single Inuit (Eskimo) origin. Approximately 138,000 Canadians claimed a single aboriginal language as their mother tongue, mainly Cree, Ojibway and Inuktitut.[3] Most of the aboriginal population is in the Northwest Territories and the western provinces; there are some 25,000 Inuit living mainly in the Northwest Territories, in northern Quebec, in Labrador, and in settlements throughout the Arctic Islands. The term "native people" includes status and non-status Indians, Métis and Inuit people. Status Indians (in the register of the 575 bands) and the Inuit (defined as "Indians" in legislation) are entitled to benefit from federal programs. The provinces provide the educational services for non-status Indians, mainly Métis.[4]

3. Statistics Canada, *Canada Year Book 1990. A Review of Economic, Social and Political Developments in Canada* (Ottawa: Supply and Services Canada, 1989), 2-9 and 2-7.
4. Canadian Education Association, *Recent Developments in Native Education* (Toronto: Canadian Education Association, 1984), p. 9.

Through the Department of Indian and Northern Affairs, the federal government is responsible for the education of status Indians and Inuit. Schooling is provided through (a) federal schools, usually on reserves and in schools that have been transferred to bands or tribal councils, and (b) schools under provincial jurisdiction where costs are paid to the province by the federal government under federal-provincial agreements. Responsibility for native education was transferred to the governments of the Yukon and the Northwest Territories in the late 1960s.

Federal schools are in every province except Newfoundland, and may be operated either by the Department of Indian and Northern Affairs or by Indian bands themselves. The program provides educational services similar to those in provincial schools, but with emphasis on native culture and languages. By 1990, 321 of the 379 federal schools had passed into band control. The majority of students attend provincial schools, either commuting by school bus from the reserve or living in residence. Through agreements with a department of education, the curriculum includes options on native culture and languages and the use of native specialists. In 1989, federal and provincial schools served 85,000 elementary and secondary school students living on reserves.[5]

Financial assistance and instructional support services are provided to more than 18,000 post-secondary students at a cost of some $142 million. This amount includes almost $15 million for native-controlled institutions and aboriginal studies programs. The Department of Indian and Northern Affairs gives some $7.3 million for cultural/educational services for 42 band-controlled centres and 27 corporate centres. These services include native languages, curriculum development and museology.[6] In 1990-91, it has been estimated, the federal government's total expenditure on all school and education-related services for native people was $850.7 million.[7]

Important issues for native people include the quality of education, local control of their own schools, programs to attract northern natives into teaching, emphasis on teaching native languages, curriculum material in various languages developed by

5. Indian and Northern Affairs Canada, *Annual Report 1989-90* (Ottawa: Supply and Services Canada, 1990), p. 19 and 18.
6. *Ibid.*, pp.19-20.
7. Canadian Tax Foundation, *The National Finances: An Analysis of the Revenues and Expenditures of the Government of Canada, 1990* (Toronto: Canadian Tax Foundation, 1991), p. 10:1.

and for native people, community involvement in education, accessibility to post-secondary education, and the creation of Indian post-secondary institutions.

New initiatives in teacher training in the north have been influenced by the pioneer work in North America undertaken by the Northwest Territories in 1968 on the concept of preparing native people for a career in teaching by adapting the traditional program to the reality of native people's lives. In 1981, the new approach was extended to include a field-based option that allows candidates to be trained without spending long periods of time away from home. In September 1990, Yukon College started a native teacher education program for students with no post-secondary background, in conjunction with the University of Regina in Saskatchewan. In this home-based program, students alternate between two weeks in class and two weeks in a school in their own communities. The college also started a full-time teacher certificate program along the same lines. In 1990, Arctic College in the Northwest Territories used the home-based approach in its community teacher education project for aboriginal language groups in the West Arctic.

More school boards across the country have introduced the teaching of a native language as part of the regular school program or as after-school classes. The Toronto Board of Education, for example, has a school in the city designed specifically for native children. Native themes are integrated into all subjects and Ojibwe is taught from 20 to 40 minutes a day. These new directions have led increasingly to criteria and programs for the certification of native language specialists as qualified teachers. An example of attention to native education is the recent strategy in British Columbia to improve native access to post-secondary education, to incorporate native institutions into the public post-secondary system, and to carry out program priorities identified by the First Nations Congress Education Secretariat, which is now the official advisory body to the British Columbia Ministry of Education. In 1987, Alberta launched its native education policy of promoting partnerships among native people, school boards and the department of education.

Post-secondary Education

In Canada, post-secondary education can be gained from community colleges (non-degree-granting) and from universities (degree-granting). Full-time post-secondary enrolment increased steadily throughout the 1970s and 1980s. For 1990-91, enrolment in the 201 community colleges and 69 universities was estimated at 856,520, a 2% growth over the previous year.

Post-secondary Financing

The post-secondary level has shown the largest growth in overall spending on education during the past few years. In 1990-91, its estimated share of the $46.5 billion expenditure on all levels of education rose from 28.5% in 1987-88 to 29.1%, or $13.5 billion ($9.7 billion university and $3.8 billion community college).[8] Post-secondary education is essentially government financed, by the provinces and territories and by indirect and direct funds from the federal government. Most post-secondary institutions must also acquire funds from tuition fees and other sources such as donations and investments.

The total federal contribution in 1988-89 was $6.81 billion. Three-quarters of this support ($5.30 billion) consisted of tax transfers (44%) and cash transfers (33%) to the provinces and territories under the *Established Programs Financing Act*, plus 1% for the official languages in education program. Direct federal support of $1.51 billion was for research (10%), student assistance through the Canada Student Loans Program (8%), and 4% for other programs and administrative costs.[9] In 1987, the introduction of a policy of fiscal constraint began to slow the rate of growth of federal transfers and set a pattern for flattening out federal support.

Since the *Canada Student Loans Act* of 1964, the federal government has guaranteed loans to eligible post-secondary students whose resources are not sufficient for the full cost of full- or part-time studies. Applications for loans are assessed by provincial governments according to criteria agreed upon by both levels of government. Under the *Act*, the federal government provides an alternative payment to Quebec, which operates a separate program. All other provinces and territories complement the federal program with various student assistance programs of their own.[10]

---

8. Statistics Canada, *Advance Statistics of Education 1990-91, op. cit.*, pp. 11 and 16.

9. Department of the Secretary of State of Canada, *Profile of Higher Education in Canada, 1990* (Ottawa: Supply and Services Canada, 1990), p. 35.

10. Statistics Canada, *Canada Year Book 1990: A Review of Economic, Social and Political Developments in Canada, op. cit.*, p. 4-13.

The amount of loans granted to students during 1990-91 was $463 million, compared to $217 million in 1981-82.[11]

Each provincial and territorial government has developed its own set of structures to govern and fund post-secondary education. Funding, which is primarily through capital and operating grants, is approved by the legislature. Financing and budget allocations for the community college sector is administered directly by the appropriate department of education or of post-secondary education. This also holds true in many provinces for funding the university sector. However, in some provinces, funding comes through an intermediary body. Nova Scotia, New Brunswick and Prince Edward Island have established the Maritime Provinces Higher Education Commission to advise the three governments. In Manitoba, funding is received through the Universities Grants Commission. Even in provinces where university funding comes through one department or ministry, there is usually a similar type of intermediary agency, such as a universities council, that acts for both the government and its institutions.

An example of the extent of post-secondary education and its financing is the province of Alberta. Its post-secondary system includes 29 public institutions: four universities, 11 community colleges, four vocational centres, two technical institutes, six hospital schools of nursing, and the Banff Centre.[12]

Universities

Any institution that has been given the power to grant degrees is normally called a university, although it may also be called a college, institute or a school. In addition to universities themselves, the definition includes liberal arts colleges, colleges of theology, and a number of institutions that grant degrees in specialized fields, such as agriculture or fine arts. The first institution of higher education was the Seminary of Quebec, founded in 1663, which was the base for the establishment of the University of Laval. The oldest English-language institution, King's College in Nova

---

11. Canadian Tax Foundation, *The National Finances: An Analysis of the Revenues and Expenditures of the Government of Canada 1990* (Toronto: Canadian Tax Foundation, 1991), p. 10:1

12. Alberta Advanced Education, *1988-89 Annual Report* (Edmonton: Alberta Advanced Education, 1990), p. 13 and 37; *Advanced Statistics 1990-91, op. cit.*, p. 29.

Scotia, opened in 1789. Canada now has 69 public, degree-granting universities, 12 of which are in federation or affiliation with another university.

The estimated total full-time enrolment for 1990-91 was 532,100 (468,800 undergraduate and 63,300 graduate students). Total part-time enrolment was 309,800 (270,000 undergraduate and 39,800 graduate students). Over half of the full-time undergraduates were women, up from 45% in 1978-79. Full-time undergraduate enrolment, as a proportion of the 18-21 age group (regardless of the students' ages) was 28.3% in 1988-89. (It was 22.4% in 1984-85.) In 1990-91, full-time university teachers numbered 37,700, an 11% increase over 1978-79. Women made up about 19% of the faculty, up from 14% ten years earlier.

With minor exceptions, the provinces have authorized the establishment and the institutional structures of universities through legislative acts. No two universities are alike, but their structure and organization are relatively standard. There are no jurisdictional hurdles preventing a student from a university in one province from entering a university in another province.

Reflecting the linguistic profile of the country, most universities are English-speaking. Of the seven independent French-speaking institutions, four are in Quebec, and one each in Nova Scotia, New Brunswick and Ontario. Two Ontario universities are bilingual and offer instruction in both English and French. Others have classes in one language only, but let students write term papers, exams and theses in either language. There are also several French affiliates of English and bilingual institutions. A number of universities offer distance education programs leading to undergraduate degrees, but only three non-campus universities serve distance students exclusively at the university level: Open Learning Institute in British Columbia; Athabasca University in Alberta; and Télé-université in Quebec.

Although every university sets its own admission standards, institutions in the same province generally have the same requirements, particularly for undergraduate arts and sciences programs. Admission is granted directly from secondary school graduation after 12 years of schooling (or the required number of credits), except in Quebec where entrance is obtained after completion of a two-year program at a cégep (college of general and vocational education plus 11 years of schooling). Most universities provide for the admission of mature students who do not meet the normal entrance requirements. Tuition fees vary from one province to another, from one university to another, and from one faculty to another. All provinces, except Newfoundland, Saskatchewan and

Manitoba, have higher fees for foreign students. Most universities offer free tuition to senior citizens.

Universities confer two types of qualifications - degrees and diplomas or certificates - at undergraduate and graduate levels. Programs leading to a diploma are not a major feature of universities and usually are for professions such as health science, agriculture, and business. A variety of courses are provided at each university, but, of course, no one university can offer all of the approximately 15,000 different courses that are now available across Canada. Undergraduate degree programs last from three to five years, depending upon the student's qualifications and whether the degree sought is pass or honours. A bachelor's degree at the honours level is required for acceptance into a master's program, which usually entails one year of study. A Ph. D., or doctorate, program normally involves two years after a master's program.

In 1988-89, two broad fields of study, social sciences and engineering and applied sciences, accounted for almost half the male undergraduates: 31% and 16%, respectively. Social sciences also ranked first for women, representing 32% of undergraduates; general arts and science programs held second place. In 1988, 103,800 bachelor's and first professional degrees were granted, 14,400 more than ten years earlier. More than half (55%) of all degrees were granted to women. (About 48% of the degrees were obtained by women in 1978.) The 16,270 master's degrees increased by 3,630. The number of master's degrees conferred on women increased by 76% over the past ten years. The growth has occurred in every field of study.

Universities are usually administered by lay board of governors and an academic senate. The most common pattern of organizational structure is the subdivision into faculties, presided over by deans. The central faculties are ordinarily those of arts (humanities and social sciences) and science (pure science, biological and physical). Faculties are traditionally subdivided into departments, which are headed by a member of the teaching staff.

Community Colleges

In the 1960s, to meet the educational demands of an exploding population and to satisfy the need for skilled technical workers, the provinces began to organize non-university education into a different system either by changing older institutions or founding new ones. The outcome was the "community college" (or cégep in Quebec), a type of post-secondary institution designed to offer a range of advanced programs as an alternative to those traditionally associated with university. The term now describes institutions that offer semi-professional career or technical and vocational programs leading to a diploma. In some instances, the institution offers university transfer programs.

There is no uniform pattern for the 201 community colleges across the country. The classification can include community or regional colleges, as in many provinces; colleges of applied arts and technology in Ontario; colleges of general and vocational education in Quebec; technical and vocational and university-oriented colleges in British Columbia, Alberta and Yukon; and colleges providing specialized training in agriculture, the arts, marine and paramedical technology.

Community colleges are based on the philosophy that educational opportunities should be extended and made accessible to a broad segment of society. Admission criteria are flexible. Secondary school graduation is usually required, but may be waived in the case of mature applicants. Tuition fees are appreciable lower than for university. Quebec's college-level system is free to full-time students. Most colleges operate year-round on a semester basis. Full- and part-time courses may be offered on- or off-campus, day or evening. The career and technical programs prepare students for direct entry into the labour force in such fields as engineering, health sciences, business, applied arts and social services. Programs last for at least one year, but more often two or three, and sometimes four. University transfer programs consist of one or two years of academic instruction that provides students with a standing equivalent to the first or second year of a university degree program. Not all programs are at the post-secondary level. They may include trades training, basic upgrading, remedial and literacy courses and continuing education and personal interest programs.[13]

In 1988-89, 317,700 students were enrolled full time; more than half of them were women. Enrolment as a percentage of the 18-21 age group rose from 17.8% in 1984-85 to 20.5%. The 185,300 part-time students in community colleges numbered 4% more than the previous year; 60% of them were women.[14]

Since the mid-1980s a number of provinces have reorganized the orientation and governance of their institutes and colleges into an integrated regional system of community colleges or learning

---

13. Statistics Canada, *Canada Year Book 1990: A Review of Economic, Social and Political Developments in Canada* , op. cit., p. 4:9.

14. Statistics Canada, *Education in Canada. A Statistical Review for 1988-89* (Ottawa: Supply and Services Canada, 1990), p. 42.

centres, as in New Brunswick and Prince Edward Island. In 1990, Nova Scotia changed its vocational schools and technical institutes to community college centres in six regions and established the Collège de l'Acadie as the province's first francophone centre.

Newfoundland and Labrador rationalized its provision of post-secondary into five new regions and opened a new campus for Labrador College that also offers a first-year university program. The *Regional College Act* in Saskatchewan gave the former community colleges more orientation to post-secondary programs and created a common first-year university transfer course. The Saskatchewan Institute of Applied Science and Technology was developed as a major place for post-secondary education.

Several jurisdictions, such as Manitoba, Yukon, Northwest Territories and Nova Scotia, have established boards of governors that have the responsibility for the overall management of the colleges.

Trade and Vocational Training

Trade and vocational education refers to programs that prepare students to work in specific trades or occupations after a relatively short period of instruction. A large number of institutions provide short-term training in practical skills that can be applied immediately in the labour market. The training varies between and within provinces and territories. It is offered in public and private institutions such as the trade divisions of community colleges, public trade schools and vocational centres. It may also take place on the job. Most programs are completed in less than a year, and courses for less complex occupations may last only a few weeks.

During 1987-88, some 233,200 trainees were enrolled in programs in public trade schools and community colleges. About 39% of them were in pre-employment programs, 21% in programs for registered apprenticeships, 6% in skill upgrading and the rest in other pre-vocational programs. Overall, 12.5% of the population over age 15 has a trade-vocational certificate. Almost twice as many men as women have completed such programs, but female participation has increased over the past years. The national expenditure on vocational training for 1990-91 was estimated at $3.6 billion, a figure that includes federal and provincial training courses, training under the Canadian Jobs Strategy Programs, and private trade schools.[15]

Most public trade schools and vocational centres are administered by a provincial department of education. They should not be confused with public vocational or technical secondary schools administered by local school boards. Trade schools may be separate establishments or divisions of a community college. Only people who have left the regular school system and are older than compulsory school age may attend. High school graduation is not usually required. Depending on the province and the trade, admission standards can range from grade 8 to grade 12.

In Quebec, trade and vocational training is organized somewhat differently. Its *Vocational Training Act* defines adult students as people 16 and older who have not attended school for at least 12 consecutive months. Most instruction takes place in "les écoles polyvalentes," which are the Quebec equivalent of high schools. Although both the regular secondary school and adult training programs are administered by local school boards, the administration of each is separate.

Apprenticeship programs throughout the country combine on-the-job training with classroom instruction. People contract with an employer to learn a skilled trade and eventually reach journeyman status. Apprentices may be registered with a provincial or territorial department of labour or manpower which sets standards and qualifications. Non-registered apprentices enter into private agreement with an employer, perhaps in association with a labour union. They are not subject to regulations established by the province or territory for that trade. In co-operation with the provinces, the federal government has introduced standard interprovincial examinations to promote the mobility of journeymen.[16]

The federal government's involvement, financially and otherwise, with manpower training increased after the 1967 *Adult Occupational Training Act* which gave it a more active role in decisions about trainees and types of training. Successive legislation, which has been worked out on a partnership basis with the provinces, has been geared to economic growth, unemployment

---

15. Statistics Canada, *Education in Canada. A Statistical Review for 1988-89, op. cit.*, p. 41; and Statistics Canada, *Advance Statistics of Education 1990-91, op. cit.*, p. 28.

16. From Statistics Canada, *Canada Year Book 1990: A Review of Economic, Social and Political Developments in Canada, op. cit.*, 4-11 and 4-12.

and job security and skill development. The Canadian Jobs Strategy of 1985 is a co-operative effort with the provinces, business, labour and community groups for training and skill development.[17] In 1991, a new arrangement for on-the-job-training subsidies, known as the Labour Force Development, was negotiated with the provinces (except Quebec) and the territories.

Continuing Education

Continuing education has increasingly become a way of life for many Canadians. A survey by Statistics Canada showed that one in five adults (over age 17 and not a full-time student) took at least one full adult education course in 1983.[18] A significant rise in participation is expected to show in a new survey. The challenge for the many providers of adult and continuing education is to improve access to even more flexible opportunities for people to learn at different stages throughout their lives. Adults return to some form of organized learning for several reasons: to upgrade their educational level, to further their education, to acquire new job-related skills, or for general interest.

These various needs are served by a range of providers. The situation is different in each province, but Canada-wide, employers are the largest providers of adult education (18.4%), followed by community colleges (17.8), voluntary organizations (16.5%), school boards (13.6%), private institutions (13.0%), universities (12.1%), unions and professional associations (8.4%).[19] The importance of adult education is reflected in the number of undergraduate and graduate programs at universities that prepare people to work as instructors, counsellors, community workers, administrators, trainers and as co-ordinators of professional and human resources development.

Community colleges, school boards and universities all offer

---

17. Statistics Canada, *Canada Year Book 1990: A Review of Economic, Social and Political Developments in Canada, op. cit.*, p. 4-12.

18. M.S. Devereaux, *One in Every Five: A Survey of Adult Education in Canada* (Ottawa: Statistics Canada and Department of the Secretary of State,1985), p. 1.

19. Canadian Association for Adult Education, *An Analysis of the Statistics Canada Adult Education Survey, 1984* (Toronto: Canadian Association for Adult Education, 1985), p. 164.

a wide range of credit and non-credit courses within their continuing education departments. Part-time learning can lead to a high school diploma or to a post-secondary degree, diploma or certificate. Credits in academic or vocational subjects can also be acquired through correspondence study, radio and television, and the application of communication technologies to distance education. Five provinces have created educational television services that offer both formal and non-formal study units. In addition to credit courses that may be applied towards a high school diploma, school boards also offer non-credit programs that include, for example, adult literacy, English or French as a second language, computer technology, and special interest subjects related to job skills and personal interests.

A major development since the early 1980s has been an increasing awareness of the problem of adult illiteracy as a significant national priority. In late 1987, the federal government established a National Literacy Secretariat as a co-ordinating body. One year later, the prime minister committed $110 million over the next five years for cost-sharing grants to new initiatives by provinces and territories and for support to voluntary and community-based organizations, labour and the private sector.

The first national publicity came from the Southam Literacy Survey, conducted in 1986, which found that more than one in five Canadian-born adults aged 18 and over are functionally illiterate in English or French.[20] These figures were borne out by a survey done by Statistics Canada in 1989 to directly assess literacy skills used in daily activities. It found that the reading skills of 16% (2.9 million) of adults aged 16 to 69 are too limited for them to deal with most of the written material encountered in everyday life. The percentage includes 5% who basically cannot read, 9% who have difficulty with simple texts, and 2% who had no abilities in English or French. A further 22% (4.0 million) can carry out simple reading tasks but lack the skills to cope with reading in a more complex context.[21]

A wide variety of programs to combat illiteracy are being undertaken by a number of agencies - from volunteer organizations to school boards and the workplace.

Several provinces have an adult equivalency diploma program that enables the adult student to undertake various combina-

20. Southam News, *Broken Words. Why Five Million Canadians Are Illiterate* (Toronto: Southam Newspaper Group, 1987).
21. Statistics Canada, *Survey of Literacy Skills Used in Daily Activities* (Ottawa: Supply and Services Canada, 1990), p. 2.

tions of courses in specific academic or vocational subjects. Other provinces provide a full complement of regular secondary school diploma programs for evening students but reduce the number of required courses to specific core subjects for each grade level. All provinces, except Manitoba, Ontario and Quebec, have instituted a high school equivalency testing program (General Educational Development exams) whereby an adult can take a series of tests and examinations (some of which take into account his or her work and life experiences) to receive secondary school equivalent standing up to the final diploma. Ontario has adopted the policy of granting equivalency credits for mature students: individuals who want to resume their education are granted credits for the learning experiences they have acquired since they left school. However, in order to obtain a diploma, they must earn at least four additional credits all in third or fourth year secondary school subjects.

APPENDIX
DEPARTMENTS OF EDUCATION

For general or detailed information about education in any particular province or territory, address the department or ministry of education of the provincial or territorial government concerned.

Alberta - Department of Education, West Tower, Devonian Building, 11160 Jasper Avenue, Edmonton, Alberta T5K 0L2

British Columbia - Ministry of Education, Parliament Buildings, Victoria, British Columbia V8V 2M4

Manitoba - Department of Education and Training, Robert Fletcher Building, 1181 Portage Avenue, Winnipeg, Manitoba R3G 0T3

New Brunswick - Department of Education, P.O. Box 6000, Fredericton, New Brunswick E3B 5H1

Newfoundland and Labrador - Department of Education, Confederation Building, West Block, Box 8700, St. John's, Newfoundland A1B 4J6

Northwest Territories - Department of Education, P.O. Box 1320, Yellowknife, Northwest Territories X1A 2L9

Nova Scotia - Department of Education, Box 578, Halifax, Nova Scotia B3J 2S9

Ontario - Ministry of Education, Mowat Block, 900 Bay Street, Toronto, Ontario M7A 1L2

Prince Edward Island - Department of Education, Box 2000, Charlottetown, Prince Edward Island C1A 7N8

Quebec - Ministère de l'Éducation, Édifice Marie-Guyart, 1035, rue De La Chevrotière, Québec, Québec G1R 5A5

Saskatchewan - Department of Education, 2220 College Avenue, Regina, Saskatchewan S4P 3V7

Yukon - Department of Education, P.O. Box 2703, Whitehorse, Yukon Territory Y1A 2C6

SOME FEDERAL DEPARTMENTS

DEPARTMENT OF EMPLOYMENT AND IMMIGRATION, CANADA EMPLOYMENT AND IMMIGRATION COMMISSION

Arrangements are made with provincial governments, private schools and industry for occupational skills and apprenticeship training. The arrangements include language training for immigrants not acquainted with either English or French. The *National Training Act*, passed in 1982, targets training adults who are or should be in the labour force for designated occupations of national importance and for those in demand. It places greater emphasis on special needs groups and provides capital for facilities and equipment.

Phase IV, Place du Portage, Hull, Que. K1A 0J9. Fax: (819) 953-7427.

DEPARTMENT OF EXTERNAL AFFAIRS AND INTERNATIONAL TRADE

The Academic Relations Division of the Department of External Affairs and International Trade aims primarily at encouraging the development of courses and centres of Canadian Studies in foreign universities. It offers awards tenable in Canada at the graduate and post-graduate levels to nationals of 21 countries; it facilitates international university contacts and co-operates with the Council of Ministers of Education, Canada, and private organizations to facilitate Canadian participation in international conferences and meetings.

Pearson Bldg, 125 Sussex Ave., Ottawa, Ont. K1A 0G2. Fax: (613) 992-5965.

DEPARTMENT OF INDIAN AND NORTHERN AFFAIRS

Through its Education Branch, this Department is responsible for the education of status Indians and Inuit from primary through post-secondary. The Department operates a federal school system on reserves and purchases services through provincial education systems.

Ottawa, Ont. K1A 0H4. Fax: (819) 997-1587.

DEPARTMENT OF NATIONAL DEFENCE

Through its Dependants Education Programs, this Department provides schooling up to and including Ontario grade 12 OAC, or its equivalent, to the dependants of Canadian Forces members living on defence stations in Canada or serving outside Canada.

Major-General George R. Pearkes Bldg., Ottawa, Ont. K1A 0K2. Tel: (613) 992-3220. Fax: (613) 992-3711.

DEPARTMENT OF NATIONAL HEALTH AND WELFARE

The Education and Training Unit, Health Promotion Directorate, of this Department is concerned with promoting health education for young Canadians and their educators. It facilitates communication between education and health professionals among the provinces and territories and provides consultation services. It also participates in developing health educational materials and encourages related research and professional training.

4th Floor, Jeanne Mance Building, Tunney's Pasture, Ottawa, Ont. K1A 1B4. Fax: (613) 990-7097.

DEPARTMENT OF THE SECRETARY OF STATE, EDUCATION SUPPORT BRANCH

This branch carries out analytical liaison and research work in the development, formulation, implementation and review of federal education policies and programs in Canada and abroad. The branch administers two programs of fiscal transfers to the provinces in support of post-secondary education and also administers the Canada Student Loans Program. Under bilateral agreements with each province, the Secretary of State contributes to the costs of developing and maintaining programs of official minority and second language education within the provincial education systems, expanding existing programs, introducing new ones, training teachers and providing bursaries and support to individual students.

Ottawa, Ont. K1A 0M5. Fax: (819) 953-8438.

SOME FEDERAL AGENCIES

CANADIAN BROADCASTING CORPORATION

With the co-operation of the provincial departments of education (particularly through the Council of Ministers of Education, Canada), universities and others, the CBC produces radio and television programs for use in elementary, secondary, and tertiary education. The CBC Northern Service offers information programs in Indian and Inuit languages as well as in English and French. In addition, both the French and English services of the CBC publish and sell selected program texts.

1500 Bronson Ave., P.O. Box 8478, Ottawa, Ont. K1G 3J5. Tel. (613) 724-1200,

CANADIAN COMMISSION FOR UNESCO

This body advises the federal government, through the Department of External Affairs, on the UNESCO program and publicizes the work of UNESCO. It also provides liaison between UNESCO and Canadian agencies directly concerned with international co-operation in the natural and social sciences, communications, education and cultural matters. The Canada Council is responsible for the Commission and provides its budget and staff.

Box 1047, Ottawa, Ont. K1P 5V8. Tel: (613) 598-4325. Fax: (613) 598-4390.

CANADIAN INTERNATIONAL DEVELOPMENT AGENCY

CIDA is responsible for operating and administering Canada's international assistance programs to other countries. It recruits teachers and other professional teaching personnel for overseas assignments and arranges training in Canada for students from developing countries.

Place du Centre, 200 Promenade du Portage, Hull, Que. K1A 0G4. Tel. (819) 997-5456. Fax: (819) 953-3348.

INTERNATIONAL DEVELOPMENT RESEARCH CENTRE

IDRC is a federal crown corporation interested in interna-

tional development. Its mission is to contribute to development by supporting the research of the developing countries' own scientists.
250 Albert St., P.O. Box 8500, Ottawa, Ont. K1G 3H9. Tel: (613) 236-6163. Fax: (613) 238-7230.

SOCIAL SCIENCES AND HUMANITIES RESEARCH COUNCIL

The objective of the SSHR Council is to promote and assist research and scholarship in the social sciences and humanities. It supports independent research, helps in and advises on maintaining and developing the national capacity for research, and facilitates the communication and exchange of research results. The Council administers a program of grants, scholarships, and fellowships and a program of international scholarly exchange between Canada and several other countries.
255 Albert St., P.O. Box 1610, Ottawa, Ont. K1P 6G4. Tel: (613) 992-0682. Fax: (613) 992-1787.

STATISTICS CANADA

The Education, Culture and Tourism Division of Statistics Canada is a national agency that stores, disseminates and analyzes national education statistics at all levels. Data are disseminated in a variety of forms (publications, microfiche, micro film, magnetic tapes and maps) and direct access to information is possible through CANSIM, Statistics Canada's machine-readable database and retrieval system.
R.H. Coats Bldg, Tunney's Pasture, Ottawa, Ont. K1A 0T6. Fax: (613) 951-9040.

COUNCIL OF MINISTERS OF EDUCATION, CANADA

The Council of Ministers of Education, Canada (CMEC), formed in 1967, is the national council of provincial ministers responsible for education. (Territorial ministers of education have observer status.) It was established with the agreement of each provincial government as a forum for consultation and exchange of information on national policy issues in education. The Council also facilitates a broad range of co-operative activities among the provinces at the elementary, secondary and post-secondary levels. Over the years, the Council has focused its work on areas such as curriculum, educational media, manpower training, student assistance, official languages in education, statistics and data.

The Council also facilitates interprovincial consultation on education-related matters that involve the federal government. This includes arranging for the participation of provincial authorities in international conferences and exchanges. Council activities are undertaken in a co-operative spirit, but provincial governments retain jurisdiction over their own education policies. CMEC activities are funded by the provincial departments or ministries of education.

The Council is composed of ministers responsible for education and it meets regularly. The main annual meeting is held in September. An Advisory Committee of Deputy Ministers of Education meets in advance of ministerial meetings to set the Council's agenda. The Council maintains a secretariat in Toronto, headed by a director general.

Suite 5-200, 252 Bloor St. West, Toronto, Ont. M5S 1V5. Tel: (416) 964-2551. Fax: (416) 964-2296.

NATIONAL EDUCATION ORGANIZATIONS

ASSOCIATION OF CANADIAN COMMUNITY COLLEGES

The ACCC (founded in 1970) is a national, non-profit voluntary association devoted to the growth, development and potential of post-secondary, non-degree granting institutions in Canada. The Association acts as a national clearinghouse of information on Canadian collegial level education, conducts research and provides liaison between and among the colleges and other related institutions, associations and organizations. The International Office, a division of ACCC, works with educators in Canada and

developing countries to design appropriate projects relevant to the economic development of those countries.
Suite 200, 1223 Michael St. North, Gloucester, Ont. K1J 7T2.

ASSOCIATION CANADIENNE D'ÉDUCATION DE LANGUE FRANÇAISE

ACELF (founded in 1947) is a national non-profit organization whose main objective is to promote and protect French language and culture in all francophone communities in Canada. It serves as a clearinghouse, does research, serves as an agent for co-operation and training among francophone educators at all levels, parents and young people, school administrators, trustees and representatives of departments of education. As well, ACELF can call on an impressive number of professional and human resources, hence it has considerable expertise at its disposal in areas related to its field of interest. It also publishes a quarterly magazine and a newsletter. ACELF produces and publishes directories and books on French language education in Canada.

Its main activities are an annual convention and annual general meeting, seminars, a national roundtable, professional development courses for staff of educational institutions, student exchanges, and a literary as well as a literacy program.

268, rue Marie-de-l'Incarnation, Québec, Qué. G1N 3G4. Tel: (418) 681-4661. Fax: (418) 681-3389.

ASSOCIATION FOR MEDIA AND TECHNOLOGY IN EDUCATION IN CANADA

AMTEC (founded in 1970) is Canada's only national association of educational technology professionals. All aspects of technology are dealt with by its members, including traditional audiovisual activities, film, television and computers. AMTEC produces a journal and conducts a comprehensive awards program. A highlight of its major annual conference is the Media Festival Awards Banquet during which awards for the year's outstanding media and computer productions are presented. The Association also has several other awards and periodically sponsors special publications and events. It does not have a permanent secretariat address.

ASSOCIATION OF UNIVERSITIES AND COLLEGES OF CANADA

This association (founded in 1965) fosters the interests of higher education in Canada. Degree-granting universities and colleges make up its membership and finance its activities. The Association co-ordinates national initiatives undertaken by its member institutions and maintains a variety of centrally administered services. It represents the concerns of the university community to the Government of Canada, to the Council of Ministers of Education, Canada, to the general public and at national and international forums. It acts as a national clearinghouse for information on higher education in Canada.

151 Slater St., Ottawa, Ont. K1P 5N1. Tel: (613) 563-1236. Fax: (613) 563-9745.

CANADIAN ASSOCIATION FOR ADULT EDUCATION AND L'INSTITUT CANADIEN DE L'ÉDUCATION DES ADULTES

The Canadian Association for Adult Education (founded 1935) provides an information service and conducts forums and conferences for those working in the field of adult education. Its principal functions include promoting innovations in adult learning, examining public policy, and linking individuals and organizations throughout Canada that are concerned with adult education. Its counterpart, l'Institut canadien d'éducation des adultes, with headquarters in Montreal, provides the same functions for the French-speaking educators and administrators in adult education.

CAAE, 29 Prince Arthur Ave., Toronto, Ont. M5R 1B2. Tel: (416) 964-0559. Fax: (416) 964-9226.

ICÉA, Bureau 300, 5225, rue Berri, Montréal, Qué. H2J 2S4 Tél: (514) 948-2044. Fax: (514) 948-2046.

CANADIAN ASSOCIATION FOR DISTANCE EDUCATION

CADE (founded in 1983) promotes and supports the effective delivery of distance education in Canada. Its primary objectives are to provide information exchange and professional development opportunities, to promote research and co-operation, and to advo-

cate the examination of policies and procedures relevant to distance education. Membership is open to all those interested in distance learning, including educational institutions, government ministries and agencies, producers and distributors.
Suite 1001, 151 Slater St., Ottawa, Ont. K1P 5N1. Tel: (613) 563-1236, extension 270. Fax: (613) 563-7739.

CANADIAN ASSOCIATION FOR UNIVERSITY CONTINUING EDUCATION

CAUCE (founded in 1954) is a professional association of deans, directors, senior administrative personnel, and practitioners whose professional careers are in university continuing education in Canada. Its objectives include the dissemination of information about university continuing education personnel and programs, the professional development of individuals working in the field, the recognition of meritorious achievement of both institutions and individuals, the representation of university continuing education in Canada (including liaison with government departments, other national associations, and organizations outside Canada), and the promotion and support of research, policy studies and other investigations into the practice and management of continuing education.
Suite 1001, 151 Slater St., Ottawa, Ont. K1P 5N1. Tel: (613) 563-1236, Ext. 270. Fax: (613) 563-7739

CANADIAN ASSOCIATION OF SCHOOL ADMINISTRATORS

CASA, successor to the Canadian Association of School Superintendents and Inspectors (founded in 1951), is a federation of 14 provincial affiliates which provides a national voice on educational matters.

It promotes and provides support for its members' professional development, makes available to its members information about professional development activities and speakers, and provides joint workshops with the American Association of School Administrators' National Academy of School Executives.

It holds an annual conference and organizes exchange programs with the U.S., the U.K., and Commonwealth countries, and

supports provincial training programs for beginning school system administrators. As well, it promotes communication and liaison with national and international organizations with an interest in education.
Suite 8-200, 252 Bloor St. West, Toronto, Ont. M5S 1V5. Tel: (416) 922-6570. Fax: (416) 924-3188

CANADIAN ASSOCIATION OF UNIVERSITY TEACHERS

CAUT (founded in 1951) is a professional association of provincial faculty associations and unions from degree-granting institutions of higher education in Canada. Its objectives are to promote the interests of teachers and researchers in Canadian universities and colleges, to advance the standards of their profession and to seek to improve the quality of higher education in Canada.
Suite 308, 294 Albert St., Ottawa, Ont. K1P 6E6. Tel: (613) 237-6885. Fax: (613) 237-2105.

CANADIAN BUREAU FOR INTERNATIONAL EDUCATION

The CBIE (founded in 1966) is the successor to the Canadian Service for Overseas Students and Trainees. Its membership includes post-secondary institutions, individuals and national and local organizations involved with education. The bureau administers education travel and exchange programs. It acts as a resource centre for foreign student advisors on Canadian campuses, and it maintains contact with federal and provincial governments to express its views and those of its constituency on policies that affect foreign students in Canada. CBIE also contracts to place foreign students in Canadian institutions.
14th Floor, 85 Albert St., Ottawa, Ont. K1P 6A4. Tel: (613) 237-4820. Fax: (613) 237-1073.

CANADIAN COUNCIL FOR EXCEPTIONAL CHILDREN

The purpose of the Council is to advance the general welfare and education of all exceptional children and youth in Canada and to disseminate information about exceptional children. The Council co-ordinates the work of its units in Canada, supports the

publication of at least one Canadian journal in special education and co-operates with other Canadian agencies and organizations concerned with exceptional children to conduct studies and publish reports.
HRC Building, 1020 Bayridge Dr., Kingston, Ont. K7P 2S2. Tel: (613) 389-5412. Fax: (613) 384-6300.

CANADIAN EDUCATION ASSOCIATION

The CEA (founded in 1891) is a non-partisan organization that serves as a central clearinghouse for national information on public education in Canada. It brings together education administrators at all levels, trustees, national and provincial organization leaders, teacher educators and others interested in education. It makes available information about innovations, current trends and policies, offering to all those interested in education an on-going program of meetings, seminars, regular publications, special reports, research and information services in both official languages.

The Association's aim is to pursue the improvement of education and serve the education community by providing opportunities to study issues of common interest; to share ideas, experiences and information; to establish and maintain linkages with government bodies, non-government agencies and individuals; to analyze trends and directions through research; and to participate in learning activities.

Suite 8-200, 252 Bloor St. West, Toronto, Ont. M5S 1V5. Tel: (416) 924-7721. Fax: (416) 924-3188

CANADIAN FEDERATION OF STUDENTS

The CFS (founded in 1981) is a national organization representing half a million Canadian post-secondary students. Its goals are improvement in the accessibility to, and quality of, post-secondary education in Canada, and in developing the quality of student life. CFS represents students' concerns nationally and provincially on student aid, youth unemployment, and government funding of education. The Federation also offers services to broaden students' educational experiences, including a work-abroad program, a national student discount program, a travel agency, a speakers' bureau and various services to student associations.

Suite 300, 126 York St., Ottawa, Ont. K1N 5T5. Tel: (613) 232-7394.

CANADIAN GUIDANCE AND COUNSELLING ASSOCIATION

The CGCA is a national professional association of persons engaged in guidance and counselling education, business and industry, public service agencies and government. It works towards the development and co-ordination of existing guidance and counselling services as well as towards improving conditions, resources, research and facilities for guidance and counselling.
151A Second Ave., P.O. Box 21027, Ottawa, Ont. K1S 5N1. Tel: (613) 728-3281. Fax: (613) 728-3481.

CANADIAN HOME AND SCHOOL AND PARENT-TEACHER FEDERATION

The CHSPTF (founded 1927) is a federation of provincial and local parent-teacher groups composed of people whose goals are to promote the welfare of children and youth, to raise the standard of home life, to foster co-operation between parents and teachers, to foster high ideals of citizenship and to promote by educational means international goodwill and peace.
323 Chapel St., Ottawa, Ont. K1N 7Z2. Tel: (613) 234-7292.

CANADIAN SCHOOL BOARDS ASSOCIATION

The Canadian School Boards Association (founded in 1923) is a national non-profit organization. Its aim is to give school boards across Canada the opportunity to share experience and expertise in providing elementary and secondary school programs of high quality. CSBA speaks on behalf of its members on federal government policy and program initiatives that affect education

CSBA members include ten provincial associations of English-speaking public school boards/school trustees and the association representing school boards in the Northwest Territories. As well, the Association has individual school board members in some provinces. It is funded by its members. External funding for research and studies is channelled through the Canadian School Boards Research and Development Trust, the Association's charitable arm.
Suite 505, 124 O'Connor St., Ottawa, Ont. K1P 5M8. Tel: (613) 235-3724. Fax: (613) 238-8434.

CANADIAN SOCIETY FOR THE STUDY OF EDUCATION

The primary objective of CSSE (founded in 1972) is to promote the advancement of research in education throughout Canada. The Society provides a forum for scholarly debate through its publications and annual conferences and contributes to scholarly exchange among the members of nine affiliated associations. The co-operating associations, all of which retain their identity within the CSSE structure, are the Canadian Association for Curriculum Studies, Canadian Association of Deans of Education, Canadian Association for Educational Psychology, Canadian Association of Foundations of Education, Canadian Association for Teacher Education, Canadian Association for the Study of Educational Administration, Canadian Educational Researchers Association, the Comparative and International Education Society of Canada, and the Canadian Francophone Association of Deans and Directors of Education.
1 Stewart Ave., Ottawa, Ont. K1N 6H7. Tel: (613) 230-3532. Fax: (613) 230-2746.

CANADIAN SOCIETY FOR THE STUDY OF HIGHER EDUCATION

The Canadian Society for the Study of Higher Education (formed in 1970) provides the means of communication among persons in academic disciplines and administrative positions conducting or using research in post-secondary eduction. Its purpose is the advancement of knowledge in the field of post-secondary education through research and the dissemination of the results in publications and learned meetings. CSSHE publishes a journal, holds an annual conference at the Learned Societies meetings each spring, co-operates in the publication of special studies and makes recommendations on developmental policy in higher education to government.
Suite 1001, 151 Slater St., Ottawa, Ont. K1P 5N1. Tel: (613) 563-1236, Ext. 270. Fax: (613) 563-7739.

CANADIAN TEACHERS' FEDERATION

The CTF (founded in 1920) receives its support from the provincial and territorial teacher organizations. It publishes re-

ports and studies, sponsors seminars on matters of professional concern, provides an information service, and represents the interests of teachers at the national and international levels. CTF is a member of the World Confederation of Organisations of the Teaching Profession. The Canadian Teachers' Federation program includes the Hilroy Fellowship Awards for innovative teaching, and Project Overseas, through which programs of in-service training are offered to teachers in developing countries. The CTF Advisory Committee on Services Involving French as a First Language gives particular attention to the problems of francophone teachers in Canada.
110 Argyle Ave., Ottawa, Ont. K2P 1B4. Tel: (613) 232-1505. Fax: (613) 232-1886.

FEDERATION OF INDEPENDENT SCHOOLS IN CANADA

The Federation of Independent Schools in Canada (founded in 1980) acts on behalf of provincial and national independent (private) school associations. The Federation's objectives include the maintenance of a comprehensive resource document on independent schools that includes the names of provincial and national contact persons, provincial regulations across Canada, provincial and national activities and major issues, and a bibliography of available resources.
Suite 440, 10766 - 97 St., Edmonton, Alta. T5H 2M1. Tel: (403) 424-7273.

FURTHER READING

Adult Literacy Canada 1990: Report to the 42nd Session International Conference on Education, Geneva, September 3-8, 1990/ Alphabétisation des adultes Canada 1990: Rapport de la 42e session Conférence internationale de l'Éducation, Genève du 3 au 8 septembre 1990. Toronto: Council of Ministers of Education, Canada, and Ottawa: Department of the Secretary of State, 1990.

Advance Statistics of Education 1990-91 / Statistique de l'enseignement - Estimations 1990-1991. Ottawa: Supply and Services Canada, 1990.

Canada Year Book 1990: A Review of Economic, Social and Political Developments in Canada. Ottawa: Supply and Services Canada, 1989.

Directory of Canadian Universities/Répertoire des universités canadiennes 1991. Ottawa: Association of Universities and Colleges of Canada, 1991.

Education in Canada: A Statistical Review for 1988-89/ L'éducation au Canada: Revue statistique pour 1988-89. Ottawa: Supply and Services Canada, 1990.

Federal Involvement in Public Education, by Ernest D. Hodgson. Toronto: Canadian Education Association, 1988.

Legacy for Learners: Report of the Royal Commission on Education. Victoria, B.C.: Queen's Printer, 1988.

Minority and Second Language Education: Elementary and Secondary Levels 1988-89/ Langue de la minorité et langue seconde dans l'enseignement, niveaux élémentaire et secondaire 1988-1989. Ottawa: Supply and Services Canada, 1990.

The National Finances: An Analysis of the Revenues and Expenditures of the Government of Canada 1990. Toronto: Canadian Tax Foundation, 1991.

The Price of Quality: The Public Finance of Elementary and Secondary Education in Canada, by Stephen B. Lawton. Toronto: Canadian Education Association, 1987.

Provincial and Municipal Finances 1989. Toronto: Canadian Tax Foundation, 1990.

Recent Developments in Native Education. Toronto: Canadian Education Association, 1984.

Requirements for Teaching Certificates in Canada/ Conditions d'obtention des brevets d'enseignement au Canada. Toronto: Canadian Education Association, 1987.

Review of National Policies for Education: Canada. Paris: Organisation for Economic Co-operation and Development, 1976.

Secondary Education in Canada: A Student Transfer Guide. 6th Edition. Toronto: Council of Ministers of Education, Canada, 1991.

The State of Minority-Language Education in the Provinces and Territories of Canada/ L'état de l'enseignement dans la langue de la minorité dans les provinces et les territoires du Canada. Toronto: Council of Ministers of Education, Canada, 1983.

A Statistical Portrait of Elementary and Secondary Education in Canada/ Portrait statistique de l'enseignement primaire et secondaire au Canada. Ottawa: Statistics Canada, and Toronto: Council of Ministers of Education, Canada, 1990.

Teaching in Canada, 1988. Ottawa: Canadian Teachers' Federation, 1988.